Triceratops
(try-SARE-ah-TOPS)

Spinosaurus
(SPY-no-saw-rus)

Kentrosaurus
(KEN-tro-saw-rus)

Tyrannosaurus rex
(ty-ran-oh-SAW-rus rex)

Dinosaurs, Dinosaurs by Byron Barton

HarperCollins*Publishers*

Library of Congress Cataloging-in-Publication Data Barton, Byron. Dinosaurs, dinosaurs / Byron Barton p. cm.
Summary: In prehistoric days there were many different kinds of dinosaurs, big and small, those with spikes and those with long sharp teeth.
ISBN 0-690-04768-1 (lib. bdg.).—ISBN 0-694-00269-0.—ISBN 0-06-443298-X (pbk.) (1. Dinosaurs—Fiction) I. Title. PZ7.B2848Di 1989
88-22938 (E)—dc19 CIP AC

there were dinosaurs.

There were dinosaurs with horns

and dinosaurs with spikes.

There were dinosaurs with clubs

on their tails

and dinosaurs with armored plates.

There were

dinosaurs with sails on their backs

and dinosaurs with hard bony heads.

There were dinosaurs with long

sharp claws and long sharp teeth

and dinosaurs
with long, long necks
and long, long tails.

There were big dinosaurs

and small dinosaurs.

There were fierce dinosaurs

and scared dinosaurs.

There were hungry dinosaurs

and very tired and

very, very sleepy dinosaurs.

Dinosaurs, dinosaurs, a long time ago.

Stegosaurus
(steg-oh-SAW-rus)
Ankylosaurus
(an-KY-loh-SAW-rus)

Pachycephalosaurus
(PAK-ee-SEF-ah-loh-SAW-rus)
Diplodocus
(dip-LAH-doh-cuss)
Compsognathus
(komp-sog-NAY-thuss)